THE TENACITY OF A SOLDIER

Lessons in Effective Leadership

ELGIN COOPER

The Tenacity of a Soldier
Lessons in Effective Leadership

Copyright © 2018 by Elgin Cooper

ISBN-13: 978-1-7328104-0-2

This book was printed in the United States of America

To order additional copies of this book contact:
LaBoo Publishing Enterprise, LLC
staff@laboopublishing.com
www.laboopublishing.com

I dedicate this book to my mother and father for instilling Tenacity in me, and to my wife for her continuous support.

Introduction

Learning from practice isn't enough; you can develop expertise faster through the "use" of practice. But if you take advantage of what others have learned, you get the benefit without having to go through the experience. Identifying goals is the start but if your goal is too high, you will determine it's just unrealistic. To the contrary, if you set your goal too low, you will assume you'll accomplish it no matter what happens. You must establish goals that are on the edge of your abilities. Not too easy. Just right. If possible, you should step away from a problem: it will allow you to learn more about the problem. A moment of silent introspection will ultimately lead to a more focused deliberation of the problem. Leaders inspire others toward common goals and never lose sight of the future. Management emphasizes how to maximize the efforts of others, towards the achievement of a goal. Managers/leaders aren't born; rather, they are made. In this book you will find examples of Tenacity that can easily be applied in all facets of management. I will offer you tools for tackling procrastination and useful insights about learning.

1 Childhood – An Introduction to TENACITY

I am the older of two boys born to Elgin and Ida Cooper. I was born and raised in Jackson, Mississippi by my parents. They were raised as sharecroppers in Mississippi during the Jim Crow era, which perpetuated peril, racism and prejudice. It was equally oppressive for African American children to obtain an education in Mississippi. It was common practice in Mississippi for black children to spend the majority of the school year working in the fields as sharecropper helpers. My father was born in Amite County, which is located in southwestern Mississippi; he had a 6th grade education. My mother was born in Sunflower County, which is in northeast Mississippi; she had a 9th grade education.

My father worked at the Jackson Country Club as a laborer. Tasked with paying all bills and providing for our family, he worked six days a week. It's remarkable that my father was able to provide for a family of four while making only $1.60 per hour, or $64.00 per week, at his retirement. My mother was a homemaker and worked part-time as a maid. My mother was the disciplinarian and matriarch of the family.

My mother continually stressed the need for my brother and I to obtain our education. She would make surprise visits to our schools to verify our classroom performance. Any areas of deficiency that arose during her discussion with our teachers would require us to stay after school for additional training and reinforcement of those specific principles. Once we returned home from school we were required to study an additional three hours daily. She emphasized that grades of C or lower weren't acceptable and wouldn't be tolerated. She disliked the image of indolent black children. She would administer punishment quickly to us for our failure to excel in education. She adapted the philosophy "Spare the rod and spoil the child." That was my initial introduction to TENACITY.

As a child growing up during the Jim Crow era, I understood that education was my route out of the racism and prejudice that surrounded me. My initial introduction to TENACITY was when my cousin stopped by to see my mother. He was en route to his next duty station. At the time he was a Captain in the Air Force, and I subsequently was told that he was not only a pilot but also a fighter pilot. I fell in love with his flight suit and those aviator glasses. I wanted to emulate him after graduating from college. After completing college, I met him again. He explained that he was retired and now working as a Flight Evaluator for the Federal Aviation Administration. He had been the Wing Commander at Langley Air Force Base, Eustis, Virginia. He would serve as a role model to me.

My next introduction to TENACITY was when my mother's oldest sister's son was accepted into the Air Force Academy, Colorado Springs, Colorado in 1965. I was naïve and too young to truly grasp and understand how difficult it was for him to be accepted into the Academy at that time. His entry into the Academy and subsequent graduation served as another role model. It also was a reminder of family pride and TENACITY. His son was recently promoted to the rank of Colonel in the United States Army.

My childhood neighborhood was a nurturing environment. My street was full of my relatives, including my grandmother (who was my father's pillar of strength), two uncles and their wives and children. You knew everyone by name on the street and the surrounding blocks. My neighborhood was truly a village in raising each neighborhood child. It wasn't hard to remember names because everyone walked to and from school. Thus, you were introduced to new friends and acquaintances on a daily basis.

It was that network of relatives that reinforced education and the necessity to obtain it and to conduct your due diligence in each of your endeavors. My cousins served as mentors and student teachers to ensure that education was a priority in my life. We were always able to seek and receive additional tutoring when necessary. Those cousins were my stability and provided a pathway and additional guidance to success. They have all graduated from college and have been successful in their undertakings.

The elders of the community served as truancy officers and urged you to achieve heights that they could only imagine. They readily explained and discussed their personal perils of growing up during the Jim Crow era. They would explain the numerous obstacles regarding racism and prejudice in providing for their families.

Lessons Learned: These oral lessons regarding slavery, racism, prejudice and the numerous hardships of sharecropping were a constant reminder that education was the only option available to young black kids. Those oral lessons reinforced trust, respect and pride in all your endeavors. They provided guidance and structure into your chosen career path, and also demonstrated and reflected the life in Mississippi and the numerous pitfalls of becoming a truant.

2 The Anger and Anguish of Black Men

As an immature teenager, I experienced the depths of failure and the difficulty of overcoming those pitfalls in life. My journey began working as a carpenter's helper. My tenure as a carpenter's helper was brief and quite painful. While nailing siding on a house I got distracted and smashed my thumb with the hammer. This abruptly ended my short career in construction.

I immediately began working at a local grocery chain. I earned additional hours at the grocer by performing the duties of custodian during the week and bagger on the weekends. I worked at the grocery chain for about six months before I was relieved of my duties. I was relieved of my duties based on the manager wanting his son to gain some experience in retail operations.

The next leg of my journey took me to the Kitty Cat Club as a server. I primarily worked Thursday through Sunday evenings. I learned the pitfalls of drinking alcohol as a server. I saw first-hand the anger and anguish of black men that have been forced or subjected to racism and/or prejudice and had to accept unfavorable treatment within their places of work. The alcoholic trance induced by consuming too much allows people to vent their frustration and anger outwardly in an aggressive manner. They considered the black night club/café/tavern a safe environment to vent this anger without any repercussions. This lesson was priceless in terms of my never wanting to drink alcohol. Another example of TENACITY.

My mother continually stressed and instilled in my brother and I the necessity to obtain an education. My transfer and subsequent enrollment at Murrah High School in 1968 became a challenging, distressing experience. It caused psychological shock and was a burdensome toil placed on me. At the time of my enrollment in high school, the grade levels were from 7th grade through 12th grade. My mother had taken the opportunity to enroll me at Murrah High School under the Freedom of Choice Act. I was one of six black students at a predominately white school, with an enrollment of over 600 students, in Jackson, Mississippi. I remember the stares, prejudice and immature gestures that were displayed daily at my fellow black classmates and me.

I was in complete shock arriving at the pristine campus of Murrah High School. Murrah had student parking and separate teacher parking. The campus was large enough to boast five football fields and additional space for three baseball fields. It also had well-kept tennis courts. The campus was enormous and had plenty of shade trees, and the grounds were well manicured. It gave you the feeling of a planned community.

Lanier High School campus was in direct contrast to Murrah High School. Lanier was the first high school built for African American children in the city of Jackson. Lanier was located in central Jackson. Its boundaries on the west and south sides were marked by public housing projects that were portraits of welfare, poverty and black pain. It had limited parking for teachers and no parking for students. It had a dirt track surrounding a dual-purpose football and baseball field. The grounds were primarily dirt and weeds that quickly overwhelmed those few patches of grass.

Lanier did have a tennis court, but it would be deemed unplayable due to severe cracking on the surface. It was apparent that substantial disparities existed in financing public education in Jackson. This contrast demonstrated the racial polarization between suburb and central city schools. A student's geographical location should not determine or limit his/her quality of education.

To my amazement, at Murrah the textbooks were new and/or current and completely different from the much older and worn textbooks at Lanier High School. I attended Lanier High School the previous four years and transferred to Murrah as a junior. It was common knowledge that the majority of the parents of students at Murrah were members at the Jackson Country Club where my father was employed. All my classes were intense and challenging, but my foundation was reinforced by the years of preparation that had been instilled in me prior to enrollment.

The prejudice was rampant, and the isolation was oppressive and equally depressing. For example, none of the white kids would sit next to me in the classroom and/or cafeteria or even talk to me. Those same students would tell my father what a wonderful guy

I was on a weekly basis. Some of my teachers would ignore me during class or simply gave demeaning responses to my questions. I would go to lunch in the school's cafeteria sitting alone and had pennies, grapes and cookie pieces thrown at me while I was eating. I would look up to see where the objects were coming from and the entire cafeteria student population was looking directly at me while they smiled and laughed. Their laughter would reinforce the racism and prejudice that I felt daily. I would constantly remind myself that my father worked at the Jackson Country Club, where most of the students' parents were members. That reminder served as reinforcement that I had to maintain my composure rather than react to those gestures, so there was not an impact to my father's employment. This was truly a demonstration of TENACITY.

Daily, I would find a large wad of chewed bubble gum with a needle or saliva in my assigned seat. I had a French teacher that would call me a "Nig wa" rather than say my name. I remember a History teacher that was a favorite advisor for those white students that displayed their anger towards my fellow black classmates and me. I enrolled in a Mechanical Drawing class in which the teacher was very abrupt in his responses to my questions. This teacher would deliberately allow his favorite white student to submit his drawings and he would not find any flaws and would give him an "A+". I would stand immediately behind that particular white student. Every time that I submitted my drawings, the teacher couldn't find any flaws, yet he would give me a "B". Those were purely acts of racism and prejudice.

Returning from lunch one day, I happened to notice three white kids peeping out of a second-floor stairwell window. Three of my black female classmates that were approaching the first-floor doorway. I saw those white individuals pour a brownish liquid out the window on them. I immediately went to the principal's office to report what I had observed. The principal instructed me that I was to enter and leave through the front door. I was amazed that he didn't make an inquiry as to who those individuals were.

My mother maintained that to achieve in life, I had to be placed in a learning environment. Since the 7th grade I would attend summer school, to advance my standing in the class. During the summer of 1969, my mother enrolled me in summer school at Murrah High School. A black classmate from Lanier High School was also enrolled in summer school at Murrah this particular summer. I discussed with him the proper clothing to wear at summer school. He decided that he was going to take a stance regarding his independence in attire. One afternoon he and I were outside discussing things that teenagers normally find interesting. The principal of Murrah approached us. My classmate happened to be wearing a pair of fluorescent lime green pinstripe slacks and a matching shirt. The principal asked him if he was going on stage to perform somewhere. This could be perceived as prejudice. I saw it as another example of my classmate's lack of preparation regarding and understanding of decorum and attire, that would have saved him from ridicule.

During my senior year at Murrah High School another black male classmate enrolled at Murrah. He went by the nickname "Squirrel" and wanted everyone, white and black, to call him by his nickname. Squirrel was enrolled in the same Mechanical Drawing class. The problem that Squirrel had with the class was that his submissions were full of flaws and errors. These errors and flaws gave the teacher inspiration to mark all over his drawings, rip it in half and stomp on it. This should have served as a lesson to ensure that your work was free of flaws and rechecked to ensure no errors were found. He never was able to successfully submit work error free during the nine-week duration of the class. Squirrel never grasped the principle of preparation and how it prevents poor performance. He never understood that becoming the classroom jester was a definite flaw in his development and his pursuit of higher education. Squirrel demonstrated the traits of an indolent African American in the South.

My student guidance counselor at Murrah told me that I wasn't college material and that I should learn a trade. However, I never lost my focus and pushed forward with my education. I enjoyed the satisfaction of knowing that I was on equal footing with my fellow white students. I was able to maintain a "B" average in such a hostile environment during my one and a half years' enrollment at Murrah High School. In January of 1970, I was forced to transfer back to Lanier High School due to the Neighborhood School Act. I was again faced with different and much older and worn textbooks. A number of those teachers at Murrah were reassigned to Lanier but retired and/or resigned and began teaching at Jackson Prep Academy (a private white academy) rather than report to Lanier High School, a black school. Those actions can be perceived as racist and those teachers were prejudiced, but it was another introduction to TENACITY.

On May 15, 1970, at Jackson State College, a historically black college (now Jackson State University) in Jackson, Mississippi, city and state police confronted a group of student protesters against the Vietnam War, specifically the U.S. invasion of Cambodia. Shortly after midnight, the police opened fire, killing two students: Phillip Lafayette Gibbs, 21, a junior pre-law major and father of an 18-month-old son; and James Earl Green, 17, a senior at nearby Jim Hill High School, who was walking home from work at a local grocery store when he stopped to watch the action. The event happened only 11 days after National Guardsmen killed four students in similar protests at Kent State University in Ohio, which had first captured national attention. College campuses across the county were in turmoil over the fresh expansion of the hated war.

James Earl Green, 17, had earlier that evening visited with me at the local grocery chain where I was working. James and I had become close friends and we discussed the protest at Jackson State College that day and our pending high school graduation. At the conclusion of our conversation James went to his job at a local convenience store. I was contacted later that night and informed that James had been fatally shot at Jackson State College. I was selected to be a pallbearer at James's funeral, which occurred a week later.

His death was perplexing because of the manner that James was fatally wounded. He was an innocent bystander that happened to be in the wrong place at the right time. I had difficulty rationalizing why a life with such potential and vitality ended on a street in Jackson, Mississippi. His death served as additional motivation and clarity in addressing your choices in life and understanding your surroundings. Your surroundings will elicit and shape the opinions of others that may unfairly judge you based on gender and race. This truly helped shape my desire to never accept racism and prejudice as barriers to success.

My parents had been raised as sharecroppers and had first-hand experience dealing with Jim Crow era racism, prejudice, and with demeaning acts and language, so they understood my feelings. I understood their rationale regarding stressing education and preparation. I learned to suppress my rage and anger and focus on achieving personal goals. My mother was a strict disciplinarian and had a low tolerance for average performance or failure. She was employed as a maid and thus refused to return home and find the house in disarray. She had dealt with racism and prejudice daily. Her response was to ensure that her children got every opportunity to be successful in their endeavors.

Lessons Learned: Your personal goals are your outlet in dealing with racism and prejudice. Your goals may be basic and rudimentary in scope but have achievable targets. Those targets become sub goals or milestones and readily identify the next steps forward. Goal setting is essential in achieving SUCCESS.

3 The Quest for Higher Education

Upon my graduation from Lanier High School, I was accepted to attend Tougaloo College, Tougaloo/ Jackson, Mississippi. Tougaloo College is a private, historically black, liberal arts institution. I recognized that my major should have been Mathematics, since I had completed Algebra, Geometry, Algebra II and Advanced Mathematics while in high school. Tougaloo College is located on the northern edge of Jackson. The campus was rustic and tranquil, yet the university was recognized for its high academic standards. Those features concealed its rich history of social commitment during the turbulent years of the 1960s. It was in the forefront of the Civil Rights Movement in Mississippi, serving as the haven for those who fought for freedom, equality and justice for African Americans. It was a sanctuary for leaders to develop strategies and implement to end the Jim Crow era.

Tougaloo College opened its campus to the Freedom Riders and many other Civil Rights workers and leaders in supporting the movement to change economic and political freedom in the state of Mississippi.

I chose Tougaloo College because of those factors aforementioned and the proximity to my parents. I was excited, looking to the future to establish new expectations and goals for my next steps forward. The Tougaloo experience created an environment for African American students of academic excellence, which was exhilarating to me. The diversity of the student and faculty was exceptional in challenging me to take advantage of opportunities.

The lessons in TENACITY were again evolving within me. I could also admit that immaturity was waging a psychological battle as well. I had registered for a class in Afro-American studies. My instructor, to my surprise, was white. This caused me some distress in adjusting to the challenges of academic excellence since my experience at Murrah High School. My next class that I was registered for was in Mathematics. To my amazement the instructor was an African American man dressed in African garb, his speech and his gestures were more on the feminine side, but my homophobic attitude hadn't evolved at that point in life. Those two instances at Tougaloo provided the impetus to seek a different environment to accept the challenges of academic excellence.

I would pick up my mother from her job on various days. She was a part-time maid and her job site was on my route home from Tougaloo. This particular day my mother told me to pick up a broom and sweep out the owner's driveway. This request was repeated several other times. I was immature and did not understand that I was only assisting my mother in completing her tasks for that day. My immaturity was reflected in my concerted effort to excel in my classes so that I could transfer to Howard University, Washington, D.C. I had fallen victim to the psychological battle within me.

I took my first plane ride to what I considered the beginning of my new life. I arrived at Howard University during the fall of 1971. I took a taxi from National Airport to Howard University. Several students standing near the former Howard University Law Library met me. To my amazement I was greeted with the following comments: "Hey brother, get out of that taxi with that white man!" I truly finally felt at home after the traumatizing experience at Murrah High School.

This was my first real trip away from my parents. I was FREE to enjoy the fruits of life and readily accepted the challenges of excellence that were presented at Howard University. I was naïve about the various pitfalls of college life. I was a newly enrolled student from Mississippi, and thus subject to the stigma that I was an illiterate and slow country boy. Those comments were hurtful, and they placed us all in a box. I readily accepted the challenge to disprove my classmates. I learned through my preparation at Murrah High School to suppress my rage and anger and focus on achieving personal goals. This was the evolution of TENACITY within me.

I was able to channel my rage and anger into achieving personal success at Howard. The diversity of the student body and faculty was a stunner. I initially felt overwhelmed with the sheer number of highly intelligent students from around the world that were enrolled at Howard. I quickly overcame my hesitancy to excel in my academics once I became familiar with the expectations of the university. I sought to disprove that I or any other student from Mississippi was "illiterate, indolent or country." The rigors of academic excellence at Howard were significant but attainable. It required diligence and determination to excel in this environment.

My parents were gleeful upon my returning home during Christmas and Spring breaks. They were fully energized by my academic success at Howard and displayed it to other members of the family. They envisioned my life as a result of the numerous hardships and acts of racism during the Jim Crow era in Mississippi that they had endured. I truly was blessed: the son who had gone up north and made it.

My neighborhood was buzzing but you could see it changing quickly. The elders were sadly dying off and their children were moving to the suburbs. These changes were causing the neighborhood that I proudly knew to deteriorate and lose its character. These changes were enormous in terms of new faces moving into the neighborhood that had a different set of priorities and aspirations. Juvenile delinquency had significantly increased, as well as crime. The neighborhood had taken a posture of "bully-proofing their property" by installing security doors and windows. This was their way of saying, "let my voice be heard without saying a word." I knew that my neighborhood would never be the same again, but I accepted the challenge of leaning forward.

I graduated from Howard University, thus making my parents extremely proud of my accomplishment. My graduation from Howard was the impetus to my niece attending and graduating with a Masters' degree from Howard. My niece continued her education by graduating from the University of Florida Law School. She is now a practicing attorney in Mississippi. My cousin, whose father attended the Air Force Academy, also graduated from Howard University. He was recently promoted to the rank of Colonel in the United States Army. These are sterling examples of TENACITY!

Lessons Learned: Graduation is only a stepping-stone in the journey of success. It is a continuing quest for knowledge and achievement. Part of my responsibility as a leader is to help others (subordinates) to succeed. I must mentor students to plan, prepare, execute, and assess well enough to operate independently. Provide purpose, direction, and motivation for them to operate in support of the overall plan of SUCCESS! I recognized that my college major should have been Mathematics. My trajectory toward success would have been altered significantly. Remember: you must be close enough to the problem to see how things work, how things don't work, and how to address any problems.

4 Leadership

'If you're not willing to risk, you can't grow. And
if you can't grow, you can't become your best,
and if you can't become your best, you can't be
happy. And if you can't be happy, then what else
is there?'
– Les Brown, *Fearless Motivation*, 2018

My growth and understanding of TENACITY was
quite enlightening. The challenges of life are sometimes overwhelming. Yet, the spoils of success are
exhilarating, which allows you the opportunity to rise
out of the grass and stand to view the forest. Success
allows you the opportunity to seek greater options
toward self-growth and financial rewards. This self-
growth was reflected in my leaning forward.

I regretted that I never enrolled in Reserve Officer Training Corps (ROTC) at Howard University. At that point in my life, education was paramount: it was a choice in life that changed my trajectory toward success. As a young man the choices that you make may result in immediate success but offer little in terms of long-term mastery of different skills in your development as a leader. You must minimize the distractions in your life in order to establish goals that are outside of your comfort zone.

I evolved and saw the military as an opportunity for self-growth and maturation. I readily accepted the challenges that were associated with my new direction of development. I understood that it would expose, enlighten and provide opportunities that could be converted in the civilian world into real time experience. I understood that just having a degree would not equate with instant acceptance into the corporate world. I wanted to pursue my commission and serve my country as a member of its officer corps. My becoming a commissioned officer would enhance my resume and increase my opportunities for success.

Basic training was a significant emotional event. I enlisted in the United States Army Reserves. I was subsequently sent to basic training at Fort Leonard Wood, Missouri. I enjoyed the camaraderie of my platoon members. This was my introduction to my drill sergeants. My drill sergeant would tell the platoon members daily, "I am your mommy, your daddy, and your brother. This training cycle will be a significant emotional event." Those words became apparent as the training cycle moved forward. I began to demonstrate the old saying that "actions speak louder than words." I was selected as a Squad Leader, which conferred the responsibility of managing ten soldiers assigned to my squad.

A young soldier must understand that he/she must develop interpersonal skills, knowledge of the squad members, and learn to work with them. While getting the job done is key, you are a soldier, thus the Army also expects you to do far more than just accomplish the day's work. You as a leader should strive to improve everything entrusted to you: your soldiers, facilities, equipment, training, and resources. I saw so many soldiers that had the leadership skills to excel but lacked guidance and motivation. Motivation is a trait that is reflected in initiative. It results in you acting on your own initiative when you see something that needs to be done. As a young soldier, you join the Army not to be bored but challenged.

I was able to complete basic training without incident. The talent potential in our young soldiers goes unnoticed by our leaders. Leaders must do a better job of advising young soldiers how they can grow, personally and professionally.

Lessons Learned: Basic training will teach you the basic soldiering skills, but that is only part of the learning picture. As a young soldier, you will learn even more on the job. You will add to your knowledge and skill-set daily. You will seek opportunities; you will always look for ways to increase your professional knowledge and skills. You must always seek opportunities for higher-level leader development. You will learn through doing; you will benefit as much from your mistakes as from your successes. Self-confidence comes from competence: it's based on mastering skills, which takes hard work and dedication. This is reflective of TENACITY.

5 Challenges: Physical, Mental, Academic and Emotional

I subsequently applied and was later selected to attend Officer Candidate School (OCS) at Fort Benning, Georgia, "Home of the Infantry". I was assigned to 3d Battalion, 11th Infantry (Officer Candidate School), 51st Company. This was an opportunity to learn the fundamentals of leadership and basic military skills, instill the United States Army values and officership, and provide an evaluation of my leadership potential. The training would be challenging.

My arrival was greeted with the majestic signage that read, "Welcome to Fort Benning, Home of the Infantry". Fort Benning is in Columbus, Georgia. The grounds were well maintained, as would be expected. I drove by the United States Army Infantry School, I was awestruck by the gigantic "Follow Me" statue in front of the building. The statue invoked emotions within me that indicated my acceptance of the challenges that awaited me within the OCS program. I understood that I must be disciplined, focused and determined to complete the program.

The Officer Candidate School was located on Riordon Street. It was directly across the street from the United States Airborne School. The Airborne School had four massive jump towers and the airborne walk, which were distinguished as a historical landmark to soldiers that had completed the course. The Officer Candidate School had, at the entrance, two large white brick columns with a black arch that read "U.S. Army Officer OCS Candidate School." My daily passage through the arch represented my continuing journey through the OCS program.

The daily rigors of OCS truly challenge you physically, mentally, academically and emotionally. Every fellow candidate and I were issued the "Follow Me" unit patch. This patch symbolized that leaders were made at OCS. Each day began with extensive physical fitness training prior to sunrise. I found the experience of marching to class daily exhilarating due to the fact, that instead of the normal drill cadences, we had a fellow candidate that played the bagpipe as the cadence caller.

The pride of my participation in this challenging environment and my left shoulder "Follow Me" patch served as daily motivation. The majority of our classroom training was conducted at the Infantry School Hall, Academic Building. I quickly realized that each candidate had truly earned and deserved his/her place in Officer Candidate School. My determination and focus allowed me to consistently perform at a high level in the pressured environment of Officer Candidate School.

The Officer Candidate School program would challenge you physically, mentally, academically and emotionally. It was extremely rewarding at the end of each training day, the evolution of your face-to-face, first-line leadership involvement with your peers. The detailed analysis conducted by the instructors and your Teach, Assess, Counsel (TAC) Officers, the individual leadership development and understanding the tenets of reducing liability as it related to various tasks assigned.

Lessons Learned: The trust and confidence of your peers and leaders are reflected in your duty assignments in the future. The reward for obtaining the trust and confidence from your leaders is your commissioning into the United States Army as a Second Lieutenant. This program merely strengthened my mental resilience and understanding of TENACITY.

6 Direct Leadership Development

The Central America War, Fuertes Caminos, Honduras, was my baptism into military leadership reality as a newly commissioned Second Lieutenant (company grade officer). I had been selected to be the first organizational unit from the state to plan for and deploy on an overseas mission to Honduras. I had the responsibility of leading a platoon of 30 soldiers into a foreign country. My mission was convoy operations, traffic control operations and base security operations. It was stressful, yet it yielded many lessons in addressing face-to-face, first-line leadership problem-solving issues and addressing the emotional hardships of my soldiers.

I understood that this was my opportunity to develop my subordinates one-on-one; they were a reflection of my higher command. I had the opportunity to be close enough to see—very quickly—how things work, how things don't work, and how to address any problems.

I was selected to take my Military Police (MP) platoon to Honduras to protect engineers. The engineers were building a road from the southern-most borders (Guatemala) to the northern border (Nicaragua). We were based out of Palmerola (renamed Soto Cano) Air Base, which is a suburb of Tegucigalpa. We were flown in on the day after Christmas and we bivouacked near the airfield. The next day we were assigned to provide security for over 500 soldiers within the convoy that was over ten buses.

My initial dilemma was the fact that those soldiers were not armed or issued weapons. I immediately dispersed my soldiers evenly on each bus to provide security. The convoy consisted of doctors, nurses, medical practitioners and engineers. The trip to our base camp took the convoy over 12 hours to traverse 200 miles over mountainous roads and small towns.

I quickly recognized the fact that rank or grade of a leader did not indicate the position of leadership. This was apparent with the sheer number of higher rank (field grade) officers that were medical personnel within the convoy. I had been empowered and given the task to provide leadership and direction as it related to the security of the convoy and human cargo. The senior ranking officer within the convoy took the position of "powering down without powering off." His position on this matter afforded me the authority that I needed to get the job done. He would check with me for an operational status update, but not so often that he would get in my way.

At the end of my deployment it was my responsibility to return those medical and engineering personnel back to Palmerola Air Base for redeployment. I was given the repeat mission of providing convoy operations and traffic control operations. The difference was that my responsibility had increased to over 900 soldiers and 20 buses within the assigned convoy.

I incurred logistical transportation concerns (vehicle maintenance) that resulted in the convoy leaving 6 hours later than directed in my operations order. I was again tasked with providing security to personnel that were not armed or issued weapons. I dispersed my soldiers evenly on each bus to provide security. The trip from our base camp to Palmerola took the convoy over 15 hours to traverse 200 miles over those same mountainous roads and small towns. The majority of the trip was done in darkness due to several convoy vehicles requiring maintenance prior to the start of convoy operations. We were able to complete the convoy operations without incident or injury.

Integrity and Ethics

As a newly assigned Training Officer, I was faced with a dilemma that involved a senior officer charging a senior enlisted soldier with assault. I was face-to-face with accusations of unethical behavior and integrity issues. As a leader you are an ethical standard-bearer for your organization. You are responsible for building an ethical climate that demands and rewards behavior consistent with Army values.

Let me provide a little historical background on the fact that commissioned officers and non-commissioned officers (NCOs) are both men and women. Commissioned officers are direct representatives of the President of the United States. Your commission serves as the legal basis for your commissioned officer's legal authority. Commissioned officers command, establish policy, and manage Army resources.

NCOs, the backbone of the Army, train, lead, and take care of enlisted soldiers. They receive their authority from their oaths of office, law, rank structure, traditions, and regulations. That authority allows them to direct soldiers, take actions required to accomplish the mission, and enforce good order and discipline. NCOs represent the officer, and sometimes the leaders. They ensure their subordinates, along with their personal equipment, are prepared to function as effective units and team members. NCOs conduct the Army's daily business. In other words, the officer manages the Army, and the NCO runs the Army.

The senior enlisted soldier had been my platoon sergeant (PS) and later was a First Sergeant (1SG). I had known this soldier for over 5 years and we had a very close management relationship. We had both experienced the laurels of accomplishing our goals of training our units to succeed in its wartime mission. Our relationship gleamed the kind of cooperation that fosters trust and makes the best use of subordinates' talents.

The senior officer was the Deputy Commander of State Military Academy. At the completion of my tenure as Company Commander, I was assigned to the State

Military Academy. I had an excellent business relationship with the Deputy Commander, yet it lacked cohesion, which was reflective during my reception and integration counseling. I understood that first impressions tend to color your personal opinion of the team for a long time. My initial thoughts with the NCO were to ensure that we were able to team-build, develop trust and ensure that we were good fits and contributed to the successes of the training year and organization.

My initial year at the State Academy was very successful and challenging. My management relationship with the Deputy Commander had grown significantly. The command climate was excellent. I understood that climate was based on the way that members felt about their organization. During the next year the organization's climate changed. Several concerns arose that year that required answering that would describe the climate:

"Do leaders talk to their organization on a regular basis?"

"Do they keep their people informed?"

"Do leaders behave the way they talk?"

"Is that behavior consistent with Army values?"

"Are they good role models?"

The NCO and I had attempted to contact the Deputy Commander several times during the week, to no avail. The NCO and I were alarmed about resources required for Non-Commissioned Officer Educational System (NCOEDS) and Officer Candidate School (OCS). The students began arriving on the day of training but were unable to receive training resources due to the fact that the Deputy had secured those items but wasn't available. Later that evening, after students were issued their required materials, the Deputy conducted an impromptu staff meeting. During this meeting several concerns were raised concerning the lack of communications from the senior management to the staff. This discussion became a hot button issue that evolved into a double standard regarding the availability of senior management to resolve critical staff issues and/or concerns. The meeting was concluded without resolution.

It became obvious that the Deputy didn't tolerate, and became visibly upset about, staff concerns regarding his/her availability. The NCO and I were standing outside the administration building when the Deputy came rushing out the door. The Deputy had accused the NCO of attempting to insult him in front of the staff. The Deputy rushed out the door in an aggressive manner; it appeared to me that he was going to attempt to physically attack the NCO. The NCO realized what was happening and stepped to the side. At the same time, the Deputy slipped as he attempted to pivot to the right. Once he slipped on the concrete he tripped on a tree root and fell to the ground. He immediately shouted that the NCO had attacked and pushed him down. Since I was standing next to the NCO, the Deputy requested that I verify his accusation. I was instructed by the Deputy to prepare a written statement the next morning regarding my observations of the attack and assault accusations against the NCO.

To the dismay of the Deputy, I reported the actual facts that occurred. My integrity and character permitted no less than the truth. My actions were later reflected on my Officer Evaluation Report (OER) in a negative rating and narrative by my senior rater (Deputy Commander). The Deputy was transferred within 60 days to a different position within the organization. I must note that my initial year rating was top block in all categories, and I was considered for early promotion to the next higher grade. The negative rating and narrative did not affect my military career. I had always been a top performer, so I understood that the negative rating was an aberration.

The Army requires leaders of integrity to be of high moral standards and to be honest in word and deed. Being honest means being truthful and upright all the time, despite pressure to do otherwise. People of integrity do the right thing, not because it's convenient or because they have no choice. You always act according to what you know to be right, even at personal cost.

Lesson Learned: My baptism in leadership was stressful yet it yielded many lessons in addressing face-to-face, first-line leadership problem-solving issues and addressing the emotional hardships of my soldiers. I understood that as a leader you must let subordinate leaders learn by doing. You must let go of some control and let the subordinate leaders do things on their own, within the bounds established by mission orders and express intent. Those events merely strengthened my mental resilience and my understanding of TENACITY.

7 Attributes of Success

Leadership is a skill that can be studied, learned,
and perfected by practice.

(Noncom's Guide, 1962)

During my 24 years of military service, it has become
quite apparent that young officers require intense
guidance to acquire those attributes of success. Each
young person has basic qualities and primary characteristics that are their attributes. You are born with
some of those attributes; an example is the way your
genetic code determines eye, hair, and skin color.
Leader attributes can be learned and can be changed.
Those leader attributes are identified as mental, physical and emotional. You must work to improve each
of those attributes. Some had parents, some may
have had mentors—an aunt, uncle, sibling, friend or

neighbor or maybe just learned through life who were their initial positive examples of a leader. Every young soldier is a leader in some capacity.

These attributes will greatly enhance your career and are the building blocks for your success. Your ability to comprehend those leader attributes will depend on your desire to recognize and integrate them into your everyday life. Every day is purposeful, not accidental. Your everyday mission requirements are opportunities to grow as a leader.

The following are a few of those leader attributes that will become an essential investment in your future:

Will – It is the inner drive that compels you to keep going when it's easier to quit. In your days as an adolescent, you wanted to explore the wonders of your surroundings. You may have learned it from others. Through their encouragement, they instilled this attribute in you. We all have experienced the fact that things go badly: when events seem to be out of control, when the plan doesn't seem to work, and it looks like you're going to lose. That's when you must draw on your inner reserves to persevere, to do your job.

Self-Discipline – This characterizes those people who do the right thing regardless of the consequences. This is an attribute that causes young people the most stress in dealing with their peers. Self-discipline doesn't mean that you never get tired or discouraged; after all, you're only human. We understand the trials and tribulations of maturation. Self-discipline does mean that you do what needs to be done regardless of your feelings or others. You must remove those toxic, negative, energy-draining people from your life to be successful.

Initiative – Is the ability to be a self-starter who figures out what needs to be done before being told what to do. As a young person you may understand what is required but lack the discipline to move forward on your thoughts due to peer pressure. You must anticipate what must be done and perform without waiting for instructions or guidance.

Judgment and Self-Confidence – Judgment means making the best decision for the situation. Self-confidence is the faith that you will act correctly and properly in any situation. These two attributes go hand in hand. Self-confidence comes from competence; it's based on mastering skills, which require hard work and dedication. Young people know their own capabilities and believe in themselves and are self-confident. Young people are constantly searching for goals that are outside of the norm because it's something they have never done. You must become a risk-taker in order to grow. If you don't grow you can't become your best. TENACITY!

Lessons Learned: Your successful grasping of these tenets will greatly improve your development as a leader. The entirety of this chapter is merely personal insights to enhance your professional growth. Whether you have aspiration to become a leader or be a more effective one, you need to understand what you are talking about. Understand when to listen to others, and when to listen only to yourself. Confidence isn't arrogance!

8 Opportunities for Success

Many young men and women will leave the military without spending enough time identifying what it is they want to do next and why. You should always focus on how the skills that were learned while serving could carry over to the private sector and how they can help you succeed.

We accept the fact that not all skills transfer equally. The same can be said of college credits. However, if you qualified for certain certification or credential in a particular industry, there is a direct and obvious correlation. Beyond that, you can rely on some of the most basic lessons learned from your earliest days of military service. These are some transferable skills:

Project Management: Corporate leaders believe that all veteran leaders are project managers based on the nature of the military. Time management is a critical part of this, which you learned from your first day in the military. Whether you are planning real-world missions, successfully meeting deadlines is stressed in all our daily activities. The sense of urgency and demand for accountability is only taught in the military.

Organizational Management: As an officer you will understand the value of wire diagrams and appreciate each person's need to have specific roles and responsibilities. You are trained to empower each other by freely delegating power, and responsibility becomes second nature, but it is not a common skill outside the military. Organizational management is critical to the success in the vast majority of missions that you will encounter—in uniform or business attire.

Personal Leadership: We all understand how important your leadership skills are in enhancing your ability to direct soldiers and/or employees. As a Company Commander or a Battalion Commander, you need to ensure your people have no problems with their pay, are making good decisions during their free time, are accomplishing the mission, and are doing the right things to succeed. You are trained to care about your people. If you truly care about others around you, you understand that together you can accomplish more. This is a mind-set that is worth its weight in gold in the corporate world.

9 Weapons of Distraction

As a newly commissioned officer in the United States Army there are strategic stumbling blocks that are located on the pathway to success. Those stumbling blocks are readily identified and can be navigated without incident. Your mind must be clear of distractions, or "Weapons of distraction." Those weapons of distraction will cause you to lose focus on what is the task/operation/mission that is to be performed. You must remain calm under pressure, "watch your lane," and expend energy on things you can fix. Inform your supervisor/boss/leader of things you can't fix and don't worry about things you can't affect.

Some weapons of distraction for a young officer include the following:

- **Education** – A young officer not completing his/her educational requirements for advancement and promotion. The military educational system provides formal education and training for job-related and leadership skills. The military system is established for you to go out and use your skills in an assignment before being considered for the next level of schooling. This is critical in developing leaders and preparing you for positions of increased responsibility.

- **Self-Control** – A leader must control his/her emotions. No soldier wants to work with or for a hysterical leader who might lose control in a stressful situation. Your maintaining self-control inspires calm confidence in subordinates, which is a prerequisite for a successful unit. A bad day for the leader should not have to be a bad day for everyone else.

During my tenure as a Battalion Executive Officer, I observed a Company Commander losing their temper and composure during a routine telephone conversation with the Battalion Commander. The call was regarding the status of an assigned task to his/her company. The conversation quickly turned negative as a result of the Battalion

Commander's request for clarification regarding responses to information provided by the Company Commander. Respecting subordinates helps create mutual respect in the leader-subordinate relationship. Mutual respect improves the chances of changing or maintaining behavior and achieving goals. The Company Commander kept interrupting and did not keep the conversation with the Battalion Commander open-ended.

The Company Commander was immediately relieved of his/her command. The Battalion Commander prepared a "Relief for Cause" Officer Evaluation Report, which served as a death sentence for the Company Commander. The opportunity for promotion had all but vanished during his/her telephone conversation with the Battalion Commander. The relieved officer never recovered from that incident and his/her career in the military was short lived. The Battalion Commander regarded the conversation as an interrogation by a subordinate.

The Company Commander lacked credibility by not providing clarity and consistency in their statements and responses. Credibility refers to using a straightforward style, and behaving in a manner that your supervisor/ boss/leader can respect and trust. You can gain credibility by repeatedly demonstrating your willingness to assist the staff and being consistent in what you say and do. Your lack of credibility will greatly influence a leader's ability to trust you.

- **Character** – What's right and motivates you to do it, regardless of the circumstances or the consequences. Making the right choice and acting on them when faced with an ethical question, whether on duty or off duty. Whether you hold yourself and your subordinates to the highest standards, you must reinforce the values those standards embody. They will spread throughout the team, unit, or organization- like the ripples from a pebble dropped into a pond.

- **Initiative** – Self-starter who figures what needs to be done before being told what to do. You must anticipate what must be done and perform it without waiting for instructions or guidance. You are entrusted with the ability to make decisions that make your leader's job easier. You should ask for advice from others with more experience or seek clarification when you don't understand what's required.

- **Maintaining Standards** – The military has established standards for all its activities. Standards are formal, detailed instructions that can be stated, measured, and achieved. They provide a performance baseline to evaluate how well a specific task has been executed. As a leader you must set priorities on the tasks. The fact that a task isn't a first priority doesn't excuse sloppy performance. If you don't know, can't communicate and enforce standards, your subordinates and you will fail in achieving the task.

- **Establishing and Setting Goals** – You must include in your daily work schedule setting intermediate goals to get the unit ready. You must involve your subordinates in goal setting. Their cooperation will foster trust and make the best use of subordinates' talent.

- **Maintaining Critical Skills** – In every field there are certain skills in which all members must be proficient. Soldiers know what they are and expect their leaders to be able to perform them. You must identify and be proficient in those critical, direct-leader skills they need to assess tactical training and set the example.

- **Physical Fitness** – All military leaders are physically fit, and they make sure their subordinates are fit as well. Physically fit soldiers perform better in all areas, and physically fit leaders are better able to think, decide, and act appropriately under pressure. If a leader isn't physically fit, the effects of additional stress snowball until their mental and emotional fitness are compromised as well.

- **Professional Bearing** – As a military leader, you're expected to look like a soldier. Know how to wear the uniform and wear it with pride at all times. Meet height and weight standards.

- **Officer Evaluation Report** – On a yearly basis your performance as a leader is evaluated by your immediate chain of command. The Officer Evaluation Report (OER) is a culmination of those aforementioned weapons of distraction. A poor performance/referred OER can/will greatly impact your ability to be promoted to the next higher grade.

Lessons Learned – The weapons of distraction will impair if not hinder your career progression. The performance evaluation of Character is best defined as: the military requires you to both *look good and be good*. TENACITY!

10 Warrior Ethos Short Stories

The warrior ethos is fueling the fire to fight through those conditions to victory no matter how long it takes, no matter how much effort is required. It requires unrelenting and consistent determination to do what is right and to do it with pride, both in war and military operations other than war. As soldiers we never give up on our fellow soldiers, and we never compromise on doing our duty.

Mission Integrity

During Annual Training, as a Platoon Leader (PL) and Company Executive Officer (XO), I was delegated the authority to ensure that the unit's perimeter was in accordance with the guidance from the commander and higher headquarters. I needed to verify that each

PL and Platoon Sergeant (PS) had a clear understanding of our mission. I had to ensure that the individual PLs developed, implemented and supervised platoon and individual training, which would ensure that all platoon members gained and maintained a high level of realism.

My platoon had the following security missions of Entry Control Point (ECP) to our unit along with Main Supply Route (MSR) security. We were instructed to ensure 24-hour security at the ECP and the verification of identity of all soldiers and VIPs requesting entry. We would conduct prone frisk of all vetted and unvetted soldiers. Those VIPs that were not listed on the access roster were requested to contact and return to higher headquarters for vetting.

We had specific instructions from higher headquarters to ensure that all security access procedures were followed. On this particular day, we received a staff visit from the Battalion Executive Officer (Bn XO) and S-3 (Operations Officer). Upon approaching the ECP, the soldiers reviewed the access roster to verify that those individuals had been vetted. It was apparent that their names had been omitted from the roster. The XO indicated that it was in error, but my soldiers refused to allow them entry into the unit's base camp. At that point the senior NCO at the gate contacted me for assistance in resolving this matter. I immediately informed the Battalion Commander of the error. I was informed to allow entry but comply with those designated frisk procedures. I reported to the entry point and informed the XO and S-3 of the procedures. At that point the XO became irate at the possibility that he/she was required to submit to a prone search. The S-3, on the other hand, was elated that the unit was in compliance and conducting security access procedures as prescribed.

The XO told me that this procedure wasn't necessary but would comply. At the conclusion of the frisk he/she informed me "my actions would not be forgotten." I informed the XO that I was in compliance with instructions from higher headquarters. The next year I was selected for the position of Company Commander along with the Bn XO becoming my new Battalion Commander. As a newly selected Battalion Commander, he/she was entitled to request compliance inspections of his/her assigned units to determine operational and procedural effectiveness.

My unit was subsequently informed and scheduled for the Annual General Inspection in 90 days. I had anticipated such an inspection, and we had thus taken the necessary steps and implemented corrective procedures. We had requested and participated in several administrative audits to ensure compliance. The inspection day arrived. What surprised me was not the depth of the inspection, but the sheer number of auditors assigned to conduct the inspection. Normally the audit team would consist of a subject matter expert (SME) and assistant from each of the functional areas. This particular inspection the audit team had been increased to over 15 SMEs to conduct the audit.

The Battalion Commander indicated that my unit's failure of this audit would surely be career-ending for me as an officer. I understood the adage "you inspect, what you expect." I was very comfortable that my staff was prepared. I had taken a hands-on approach to demonstrate my willingness to assist my subordinates and always being consistent and honest in what I said and did. I understood that honesty was the foundation of trust. Lies are catastrophic trust-breakers of relationships. No one trusts a liar.

To the amazement of the Battalion Commander, my unit successfully passed the Annual General Inspection in all categories. I had continuously emphasized to my subordinates that, in their daily work, they were always to set intermediate written goals to get the unit ready. My subordinates and I understood that we were building a team. Mutual assurance is always the necessary link that will help an organization accomplish the most difficult tasks.

Delegating Authority

As a leader you should involve your subordinates by delegating the authority to solve problems and make decisions without clearing them through you. A mature leader with experienced subordinates should always want to create learning experience for their subordinates. You just need to give them authority to make decisions, the necessary resources, and a clear understanding of the mission. You are ultimately responsible for what does or does not happen, but in delegating you hold the subordinate leaders accountable for their actions as well.

On several occasions I was designated as Acting Company Commander as a 2nd Lieutenant and Platoon Leader while the actual commander was tasked with other duties. On this occasion during Annual Training (AT), the unit was scheduled to participate in the Army Training and Evaluation Program (ARTEP) and receive an evaluation. The unit was evaluated to verify that it was performing collective tasks to support our mission. This assignment was equally challenging. As the Acting Commander, I was now responsible for 150 soldiers.

My daily task was to ensure that my platoon leaders knew the mission, intent, purpose, direction and motivation. This same information was given to the First Sergeant who addresses the NCOs to ensure support for the exercise or operation is feasible and suitable. I would emphasize the necessity of rehearsal. Rehearsal would allow subordinates to see how things are supposed to work and build confidence in the plan for both the soldiers and leaders. A simple walk-through helps subordinates visualize who's supposed to be where, doing what and when. Rehearsals help soldiers remember their responsibilities.

My platoon leaders and NCOs were encouraged to adapt and improvise in situations that changed drastically. Daily I would provide an assessment of their performance in the After-Action Reviews. This assessment was straightforward feedback. I would tell them where and what were their strengths; and let them know where they could improve. I would direct them to come up with a plan of action for self-improvement and offer my assistance.

If the platoon leaders are competent, and their subordinates trust one another, those members and the larger unit will hang together and get the job done. Soldiers who belong to a successful team look at nearly everything in a positive light; their winners' attitude is infectious, and they see problems as challenges rather than obstacles. Subordinates learn to trust their leaders if the leaders know how to do their jobs and act consistently.

At the end of the ARTEP evaluation period, an evaluation was prepared regarding the performance of the unit. The unit was evaluated as "Trained" (T's) in all areas that were evaluated. We were the first and only unit to receive such an evaluation. My trust in my subordinates was evident, as was their trust in the capabilities of their soldiers. As a leader you must keep your subordinates informed because doing so shows trust, because sharing information can relieve stress, and because information allows subordinates to determine what they need to do to accomplish the mission when circumstances change.

Privileges of Rank

As a newly appointed Company Commander as a 2nd Lieutenant, I was selected to a position that is normally reserved for senior 1st Lieutenants or Captains. The position of Company Commander is a position that is normally reserved for senior 1st Lieutenants and/or Captains. In the United States Army, a captain with three to six years of service as an officer usually holds the position of Company Commander. A senior first lieutenant may be selected for company command in lieu of an available captain. As the commanding officer, he or she exercises full command and control over the unit and may exercise non-judicial punishment authority over unit personnel. A company command is usually considered a prestigious assignment and important in career progression if an officer hopes to attain higher rank. A typical tour of duty for this assignment is 18 to 24 months in the active duty component and 24 to 36 months in the reserve component.

As a newly selected Company Commander in the United States Army Reserves, I was the junior officer since I was a 2nd Lieutenant and the other two company commanders were Captains. Each Company Commander had been tasked by the Battalion Commander to conduct reconnaissance missions to identify potential locations for our respective companies. We were instructed to report back to the Battalion's Operations Officer (S-3) and staff with coordinates for the potential location of our units.

My First Sergeant (1SG) and I had reconned an area that we recognize as having great potential. Once we alerted the battalion operations officer of the actual coordinates, the Battalion Commander was in the vicinity and decided that location would serve as the headquarters for his staff. We were instructed to continue our reconnaissance mission in an effort to identify another location for our unit.

Our recon mission had now expanded to 20 miles from the location of battalion headquarters. We searched for over several hours before locating a site that was large enough and suitable for a company size element. We identified a second potential location for our unit. Once again, we contacted the S-3 with the coordinates. Those coordinates were approved, and we were instructed to report to a specified location for a coordination meeting with the Battalion Commander and the staff.

The Executive Officer (XO) conducted the coordination meeting. The XO requested a status on the reconnaissance mission of each Company Commander. It was determined that another Company Commander had not identified a suitable location for their unit. The Battalion Commander instructed me to relinquish my location and provide those coordinates to that Company Commander that had not located a suitable location. I was instructed to continue the next morning with my search for a suitable location.

The next morning the 1SG and I began our search again. We discussed the specifics of the coordination meeting that had taken place the prior evening. It was discovered that the battalion headquarters location did not have adequate drainage, and thus large mud puddles were present. After several hours of searching we identified an area that had high ground, excellent drainage and overhead cover. The area was located about 1/2 mile off the Main Supply Route (MSR). Those provisions would be extremely attractive to the battalion staff due to the size of the site, and adequate for the numerous sectional activities that required vehicular traffic. The site offered additional training space for concurrent training.

We understood our requirement of contacting the battalion operations officer regarding the specific location and coordinates. Our concern was that the Battalion Commander and the staff would take this site before. Thus, we devised a plan to ensure that during the battalion staff's visit the numerous benefits of this site would not be revealed. The Battalion Commander made the cursory visit to the site and readily approved the location.

After several days of torrential rains, the battalion headquarters area became a massive mud pit due to poor drainage and the amount of vehicular traffic within the compound. The Battalion Commander made another VIP site visit to my location along with a General Officer. The Battalion Commander jokingly expressed his regret to me in private, the irony being his staff's failure to take a closer look at the benefits of my area. He stated that I had the better location and that he would exchange, but the move was too labor-intensive and time-consuming.

We were able to perform all tasks in an outstanding manner based on availability of vehicles and strong troop morale. Soldiers will always perform better in conditions that don't pose physical and/or mental hardships. You are always taught to ensure that your soldiers have a warm meal or something warm to drink at the conclusion of their assigned duties. The welcoming thought of food and drink is reflective of your caring for your troops well-being.

The Farm Club

An officer is only as good as the team of soldiers that he/she leads. Those soldiers will determine whether the leader is successful or unsuccessful. I was very fortunate to serve a dual role as a Line Company Commander and Junior TAC Officer at the State Military Academy. Those assignments separately are extremely challenging and require an enormous amount of time and energy to ensure success. The task of balancing both was driven by my motivation to be a successful Company Commander and my dedication to those Officer Candidate students.

My tenure as a Line Company Commander was highly successful. I emphasized to my subordinates that confidence comes from training under conditions more strenuous than they would likely face otherwise. This same principle was applied to the students at the Military Academy. The results at the Military Academy were demonstrated in the will of each of the Officer Candidates (OCs). Those OCs were required to persevere despite limitations, setbacks, physical exhaustion, and declining mental and emotional reserves. They had to demonstrate their ability to energize their fellow Candidates to push through confusion and the various hardships of success.

Those OCs that completed the Officer Candidate School program were newly commissioned energetic young officers. Their youth was quite refreshing, but their lack of experience was recognized in their limited knowledge of establishing and understanding war fighting priorities. The Battalion Commander concurred that additional training in those areas would make those officers better equipped to handle time management. I was tasked with developing a program to establish priorities. I had an excellent team of Platoon Sergeants that understood our intent and assisted in developing several leadership scenarios. Those scenarios would enhance and reinforce those principles of establishing priorities and time management. The unit was a sterling example of NCO-driven leadership. Several of those Platoon Sergeants later reached the rank of Sergeant Major.

As a Line Company Commander, it became apparent to my subordinate staff and I that we were training young officers that would be immediately reassigned. Those young officers would be reassigned to other unit vacancies every six months at the end of our training cycle. I requested a meeting with the Battalion Commander to express my frustration regarding this dilemma, I was told by the Battalion Commander that "you train them, and I farm them out to my unit vacancies". I didn't understand that comment but after additional discussion with the Battalion Commander it became clear The comment was a reference to the price of my success. My unit had been highly successful in accomplishing all performance indicators. Those young officers that were assigned to my unit were displaying intense dedication, creative thinking and innovative problem-solving abilities. The overall performance of the battalion improved dramatically with the successful infusion of those young officers.

Success does not happen by accident. After all, adults don't make excuses. Only children do that!

Your success is driven by four factors that make a trusted leader. Those factors are: Honesty, Reliability, Competence and Compassion.

You must let your subordinates know what to do and why. You must ensure that you have positive communications to reinforce trust.

Order of Merit List (OML)

As a Battalion Executive Officer, I had planned and implemented successful deployment operations to Germany, Italy and Panama. I was considered to be the "golden boy" within the organization. Those high-visibility missions raised my standings within the organization and placed my name at the top of the Order of Merit List (OML) for pending selection as Battalion Commander. The OML was comprised of all eligible O-4s (Majors) officers within the organization. Those individuals listed had demonstrated promotion potential to the next higher grade and battalion command consideration.

A selection board was identified and formed of three senior officers and a recorder. Those individuals were tasked with reviewing the military personnel records of those persons listed on the OML. Those board members would rank them for consideration for upcoming vacant Battalion Commander position. The board rankings would be sent to the Commanding General for his/her approval. Should the General disagree with the recommendation, additional guidance would be given to the senior board member. This guidance would immediately be incorporated into the selection process.

Until you as a leader reach the highest levels, you cannot staff positions and projects as you prefer. The Commanding General has not only the authority but also the responsibility to pick the best for their staff. The staff chosen will reinforce the intent and vision and ensure the institutional success.

The Commanding General finally approved the selection board nomination after several recommendations were submitted over an 8-hour period. It was my understanding that my name was submitted to the Commanding General several times as their selection. My non-selection as Battalion Commander was an extremely tough pill to swallow but I understood and recognized the tenets of the warrior ethos. The warrior ethos kept me laboring for a short period of time without the recognition that came to some of my associates. I was alternatively selected as the Provost Marshal's Operations Officer for the Brigade.

I accepted my new challenge and excelled in that position. I developed and implemented an improved organizational inspection program and improved contingency planning for emergency support of civil authorities. I worked as a cooperative partner of the S-3 in planning and evaluating training and providing command and control during missions. My performance was more gratifying based on the overall performance of the Provost Marshal Operations section and the organization.

Selection to the Pentagon

The success of the Army in staffing, training, and equipping combat and support forces to the high degree of proficiency needed to deter or to defeat potential enemies must be matched by the Army's ability to mobilize, deploy, and sustain those forces in the field. Mobilizing for war or national emergency involves planning and continually refining the policies and procedures to ensure that adequate manpower and logistics arrive in theater at the required place and the proper time. Included in the mobilization process are the obligation to support and provide adequate manpower through the use of the augmentation and pre-assignment programs as well as the Retiree Mobilization Pre-assignment and Recall Program (recall program); participating in and preparing for mobilization exercises; and improving mobilization and training bases.

The Retiree Recall Program allows soldiers with 20 years of service to volunteer to return to active duty and reapply in certain high-demand specialties. I had retired from the United States Army Reserves in 2004 at the rank of Lieutenant Colonel. I applied for the program in 2008 and was selected and accepted in 2009 into the program and mobilized for Operations Enduring Freedom. I was assigned to the Office of Deputy Chief of Staff, G-3-5-7, Strategic Plans and Policy, Global Force Management Division, Executive Officer (XO) position at the Pentagon.

I had the honor and privilege to serve as the XO of the Global Force Management (GFM) Division for two years. During this mobilization I was able to change my focus as a Reservist from short-term to future focus of an active duty staff officer. You are required to focus on the wider impact, and long-term effects. Your communications are not only within the organization but also to a large external audience that includes the political leadership, media, and the American people. As the XO, my responsibilities included selection and management of the staff. You should always seek to place the right people in the right places, balancing strengths and weaknesses for the good of the country.

I understood the necessity to ensure that the staff was receiving challenging problems to solve. We are required to build the attitude that we can overcome any obstacle. We were forced to address problems with restricted time and resources, thus it improves the staff's confidence and proficiency. As a leader you recognize that planning, preparing, executing, and assessing are always continuous. Leaders always keep one eye on tomorrow. There's always another mission about to start, and still another one on the back burner.

Lessons Learned: As a leader you must ask your subordinates for input, information, and recommendations, but you will make the final decision. Leaders understand that subordinates work hard and fight tenaciously when they're well trained and feel they are part of a good team. You should allow your subordinates to assist in the creation of a plan, which means that plan becomes—at least in part—their plan. Their ownership creates a strong incentive to invest the effort necessary to make the plan work. This ownership is called team building. The leader alone is always responsible for the quality of decisions and plans. The warrior ethos is a stern reminder of TENACITY.

11 Leader Development

Senior NCOs

The adage has it that NCOs are the backbone of the Army, train, lead, and take care of enlisted soldiers. I differ with that adage because as a young commissioned officer, your best role model is your platoon sergeant. The knowledge that he/she has regarding your assigned soldiers is priceless. Their approach to working with their leader is sharing knowledge. You need to know what to do and why. Leaders who communicate openly and genuinely reinforce team values, send messages of trust to subordinates, and benefit from subordinates' ideas. In other words, the officer manages the Army and the NCO runs the Army.

As a newly commissioned officer, your mentality is that "I'm in charge." That's your biggest mistake, because you may have completed your civilian educational requirements and those initial military branch qualification courses, but you are viewed as an intern in a uniform with a gold bar. Your platoon sergeant will serve as your mentor for your first three years. Their guidance does provide your introduction to leader development. Their message to you will be purposeful, flexible, respectful and supportive. Senior NCOs such as the platoon sergeant have extensive experience in successfully completing missions and dealing with enlisted soldier issues. A positive relationship between officers and NCOs creates conditions for success.

Your belief and trust in your subordinates will allow team identity to come out of mutual respect among your soldiers and a trust between you and your subordinates. The bond between you and your subordinates likewise springs from mutual respect as well as from discipline. Discipline is the willing obedience of subordinates who trust their leaders, understand and believe in the mission's purpose, value the team and their place in it, and have the will to see the mission through. This form of discipline produces individuals and teams who come up with solutions themselves in the really tough moments. These solutions are successful in accomplishing the mission.

Your success can be defined as the accomplishment of an aim or purpose. Once you understand the intent of the organization, with the help of your team of subordinate leaders and staff, goals are established and frame the organizational leader's intent. Your success in mission accomplishment is defined by the formulation and analysis of your subordinate team. Success is no accident.

Senior Officers

An officer is a member of the armed forces or uniformed service who holds a position of authority. The term "leader development" defines your relationship with a senior officer to help guide you as a less experienced or less knowledgeable junior officer. The senior officer has expertise in a certain area. Leader development focuses on your growth and development as an officer. The mentor/leader is a highly successful senior officer who is a source of wisdom, teaching, and support. The mentor/leader looks for junior officers who are already intrinsically motivated towards self-improvement. The mentoring must occur outside the chain of command to prevent the perception of favoritism.

As a junior officer you must demonstrate the ability to plan, prepare, execute, and assess well enough to operate independently. Those attributes are essential in your leader development. You must always treat people with dignity and respect. The establishment of high standards is a requirement. You must maintain the standard to ensure that everyone in your organization is accountable for maintaining them. You must mentor, evaluate, and recognize your team members honestly and fairly.

As a junior officer, I was selected and had an opportunity to be mentored by a senior officer. The experience was awe-inspiring and exhilarating. I never felt that my performance merited my selection. I remembered that sage advice of my platoon sergeant to "trust my subordinates" and each assigned mission would be accomplished. I was a leader of a platoon. I had been given the additional duty of serving as a Junior TAC (Teach Advise Counsel) Officer at the State Military Academy. My performance at the Academy had demonstrated to the Commandant of the State Military Academy that my career potential was enormous.

The senior officer suggested that he/she wanted to serve as my mentor. Those mentoring sessions were conducted off-site or at their place of employment. Our conversations would revolve around my motivation, career aspirations and organizational positions. I was given a written organizational structure regarding rank and organizational assignments and association affiliations that would enhance my career potential and aspirations.

Mentoring is a gift that is earned and requires that you demonstrate that you are self-motivated. Your mentor is underwriting your learning efforts, projects, and your ideas as a rising leader. Your mentor will ensure that you are accountable by setting actionable long-term and short-term goals. Those goals will benefit your professional development and will define the progress of your mentoring relationship. You as the mentee will receive the gifts of knowledge-sharing, leadership development, and skill development. Mentoring simply means to give the right people an intellectual boost so that you can make the leap into operations and thinking at the highest levels. You must be a teachable mentee! You can be that person, but it requires zeal and passion for success. You are that person!

Lessons Learned: Millennials are the target generation that corporations are chasing. You are the ones to shape the workplace of tomorrow. You are demanding more from the organization. You are looking for the chance that will give you an opportunity to develop, thus avoiding being placed in a non-developmental box. Mentoring affords you the opportunity to feel as though you are even more a part of the organization and can ultimately increase organizational loyalty.

12 Molding the Next Generation

"The discipline which makes the soldiers of
a free country reliable in battle is not to be
gained by harsh or tyrannical treatment. On
the contrary, such treatment is far more likely
to destroy than to make an army. It is possible
to impart instruction and to give commands in
such manner and such a tone of voice to inspire
in the soldier no feeling but an intense desire
to obey, while the opposite manner and tone
of voice cannot fail to excite strong resentment
and a desire to disobey. The one mode or the
other of dealing with subordinates' springs
from a corresponding spirit in the breast of the
commander. He who feels the respect which
is due to others cannot fail to inspire in them
regard for himself, while he who feels, and hence

manifests, disrespect toward others, especially his
inferiors, cannot fail to inspire hatred
against himself."
– Major General John M. Schofield in an address
to the Corps of Cadets, August 11, 1879.

As an officer and leader of soldiers, I wanted to train
soldiers to effectively play a role in becoming a cohesive team. I did not want soldiers that didn't project a
high level of competence, confidence and fitness. I had
been a highly successful Platoon Leader. I understood
those characteristics that I wanted in those young soldiers. I was requested and selected to become a TAC
(Teach, Advise, Counsel) Officer at the State Military
Academy while I was a Platoon Leader. As a Junior
TAC Officer, my duties would require me to train,
develop, and evaluate an Officer Candidate's potential to serve as an Officer. As a TAC Officer, I would
know Candidates better than other cadre members
and would be able to exert the most influence on their
leadership development. I was expected to guide OCs
to develop self-confidence, stamina and endurance,
effective time management, self-discipline, attention
to detail, and other highly desired leadership qualities.

I was to set a positive example and be that role model for OCs.

I stated to those OCs, "I truly hope to mold the next generation of officers for the organization and the Army". I expected that assignment to be demanding yet rewarding, with the expectation to eventually rejoin the organization to further my contributions to the Army's mission. I was given an opportunity to train and mentor the next generation of officers and share some of my experiences. I understood the challenge that had been bestowed on me and those expectations associated with the task. I recruited and graduated the largest OCS class in the history of the State Military Academy.

I was keenly aware that I was truly the deciding factor in whether a candidate became an officer or not. I was an agent of the United States Army, affecting the future of the Army based on the caliber of officer that I allowed to graduate into the force. I hoped to establish a standard of excellence in every facet of becoming an officer. You must train them to standard to prepare them to take charge and lead their soldiers into combat and perform at their highest state. Your training plan has already been prepared, but you must add value to the OCs experience by sharing your experiences and ways to set them up for success. You are that example of what an Officer should look like and how they should act.

You must accept that you are that role model. The duty is challenging, but it is worth it in the end. Your selection for the position of TAC Officer speaks volumes regarding your potential as not only a leader, but as a trainer, advisor, mentor and more importantly an agent for the United States Army. I later became the Senior TAC and then the Training Officer at the State Military Academy. I understood that the following would continue the trajectory of my career. Those three things are:

The necessity to continually set written goals

The power of association

The thirst for personal leadership development

Lessons Learned: Are you that person who likes formulating the big picture and directing moving pieces? The expectations are greater, but so are the rewards at the conclusion. You must readily accept full responsibility for the performance of the work unit or group. You are that one who must make it happen. Whether it stems from your belief or because your job requires this of you. No matter how great you are as a human being, your effectiveness is ultimately defined by the results of your team.

13 Favorite Quotes

The following are my own quotes, which my former students will fondly remember from their tenure at the State Military Academy.

Students are required to learn specific quotes daily.

Candidate, stimulate your brain!

Students must demonstrate confidence in reciting requested information.

Candidate, make my heart pump!

Students must be physically fit to complete the program.

Candidate, I'm going to turn you into a — pound sweat bubble!

Students are required to sit in an imaginary chair against the wall. This is done to persuade those students to commit to memory the daily-required knowledge.

Candidate, have a seat on the wall!

Students are required to commit Schofield's Definition of Discipline to memory.

Candidate, let me hear Schofield's Definition of Discipline!

Students are expected to recite information in a quick and boastful manner.

Candidate, blow it out!

Students understand that this command is to assume the pushup position.

Candidate, assume the position!

Students understand that this command is to begin pushups.

In cadence exercise!

At the end of disciplinary physical exercise, the students would chant:

Sir, thank you for mentally and physically conditioning my mind and body!

Students are required to learn daily motivational quotes.

Candidate, thought for the day!

Students are required to snap to attention and pop with their salutes and facing movements.

Candidates, pop and snap!

Students are taught time management; thus, they are allowed to eat at the rate of the following:

Three chews and a swallow!

Students can sit in the first six inches of a chair while eating in the dining facility.

Candidates, first 6 inches of the chair!

Once a student declares he/her can't complete the program.

Candidate, you are a DOR (drop on request)!

Once a student completes his/her DOR packet.

I will give you an apple and a comic book. So, when I hit the ejection button you will have something to eat and read on your way back to your unit.

Students are to ensure that their uniform is free of loose threads and unbuttoned pockets.

Candidate, this isn't a rappelling course! You have several ropes hanging off your uniform!

Excuses are not tolerated.

Candidate, the maximum effective range of an excuse is ZERO!

Students must always maintain military bearing.

Candidate, stop the pimp strutting!

Students are always aware that they may be identified to perform an additional task.

Candidate, leave the mess hall!

Taller students are always required to stoop down (at modified position of attention) so that I may look them in the eye, when spoken to.

Candidate, drop down to my level!

Students are reminded that the program isn't for everyone and those that graduate will be reminded of the following:

Candidate, you will bend but never break!

Lessons Learned: As a leader you feel pride when the group succeeds during stressful and challenging periods. As a leader you must display and require responsible behavior from yourself and your subordinates. This behavior is what enables you to have maximum influence. The combination of responsible behavior with responsible attitude gives you influence, which accelerates your growth as a leader.

Afterword

This book was a series of stories of my personal growth and how Tenacity has guided me. These examples will serve as building blocks in defining Tenacity, which is the ability to persevere in the face of obstacles. We all are born with the ability to learn and are taught to do the right things. As a leader you will establish direction, build an inspiring vision, and determine where you need to go to "WIN" as a team or an organization. In determining the direction, you must use your management skills to lead and guide your personnel to the right destination. The route that you take to arrive at the goal should be efficient and a smooth transition. As a leader, you are proactive- problem-solving, looking ahead, and NOT accepting the status quo. You are that manager/leader that can manage the delivery of the vision, either directly or indirectly, and build and coach your teams to make them even stronger.

You are that effective manager/leader that has those aforementioned tenets of SUCCESS- I wish you well on your journey!